Compilation of Poems & Prose

By

George Kusimo

AF445785

Entitled:

D.A.A.T.I

Desire,

Ambition

&

The Inmate

D.A.A.T.I

Desire, Ambition & The Inmate

Copyright © 2021 George Kusimo

No part of this publication may be reproduced, distributed or transmitted in any form or by any means; including photocopying, recording or other electronic or mechanical methods, without the prior written permission of the publisher; except in the case of brief quotations, embodied in reviews and certain other non-commercial uses permitted by copyright law.

Contents

8

Desire

Venus

Venus, Venus, my phenomenal Venus;

How I long to be your Mars,

How I ought to be your Mars.

Concur the Planets and Stars whenever they've seen us;

Talk together, walk together - yet linger apart.

Away from you, my essence is sore in heart,

Exploits with you are all I chart.

Rejoice on horse and carriage or mule and cart;

From the median of vision,

To the frontiers of imagination,

Via whichever medium,

Seeks our union's manifestation.

Sauntering through the space of time,

I'm one with you, you're mine - you're mine.

Deliver me from evil; into the arms of my Venus,

I pray and beseech You, dear sweet Jesus.

Time & Again

Time & again, time & again;

I'm the pupil, in subject of sight,

My favorite teacher, time & again.

I enter the ether, she's all I consume,

Red carpet beneath her, time & again.

O' won't you see keener - ebony pupil;

Focus your retina, time & again.

The shade of her iris, whenever her eyelids

Are equidistant, it brings out her two lips,

Time & again.

Her mahogany dermis, so velvet with purpose;

Do I deserve this - so farouche & courteous,

Time & again.

As I look upon her, time & again;

I sit back & wonder, of lightning & thunder;

Coursing in neural pathways time & again.

Permeates me, like nose & perfume;

I'd desire to court her, time & again.

Conversing, she senses my aura,

Time & again, time & again.

Smile

In he strolled, late as usual.

There she sat; as normal, so regal.

Graft meant his attire was simple;

Hers were Vogue, her face - no pimple.

Sat he there, behind the clan.

Fiddles with hair, her eyes did pan.

Or so he thought, concurrent of plan.

To say thanks; pondered, how she can.

Finally! Opportunity to engage and greet.

Both stood, obstructed by crowd and seat.

Their objectives plain yet discrete.

Palms held, as their eyes did meet.

Voiced she, fervent words of appreciation.

Her countenance, catalyst of his elation.

Sent her a gift, earlier on received.

Doubts of fondness - she now believed.

His were, modest words of delectation.

As he captured her lineaments' animation.

This occurrence, long since conceived.

His plan, her smile - at last achieved.

Silhouette

Whence comest thou, O' Apparition?

Stay modest how, with thine attributions?

Sought thee I, to no fruition;

All mine days held mere illusions.

Yet a lad, a Mirage of mine dreams;

Enchanting Silhouette, of virtues supreme.

They camedst, thus I formed ye within.

I failed, as my beguile measured umpteen.

Thine absence, struck mine heart with bedlam.

The consequence, my dimming of headlamps.

Indifference ensued, from hoping headlong.

Patience; the virtue, ought been my teflon.

Surely, thou makest this statement.

Elegantly arraigned in pink raiment.

Gliding akin to angels in movement.

Here thou art, amidst mine presence.

Voice of an Angel

There lies a way in - through your heart, to a path which transcends your anatomy, uninterrupted as it perforates your soul; to the very core of your essence, antecedent to encompassing its substance - which can't be deduced by mere sense.

Should you be found wanting in AWOL at my deliverance, your incarceration is entailed in my awe, my splendor; you'd be futile to stonewall my percolation, fathom me - I've been mastered by my Vendor.

Kindled from abdomen, calligraphed by diaphragm, as a Phoenix up through the larynx, soaring into the atmosphere, proliferating the ether; vibration of particles, agape[ing] your mandibles.

Intangible waves; white water rafting tunnels of canals, besieging your eardrums. I dare you to withstand this nth form; before transmuting into its breath taking, heart capturing, soul rendering, fantasy evoking uniform. Be sure to appreciate my Vendor, when you retrieve your sensors; this wave's on the way that lies in - through your heart.

The Filly, The Mare & The Unicorn

Me, Myself and I;

Rooted together in a cerebral quagmire,

As three genes. One, true; other twain - lie.

The Colt, The Stallion and Sire.

Entwined in subsist, hitherto experience;

Given metamorphosis, pivots on expedience.

Alternate aftermath equates 180 grievance.

Comprehension snagged by equine opulence.

A thing of beauty 'I' couldn't look beyond.

Strutting towards 'Me', was this Unicorn.

Another gene's cause, worth doting on,

Other than 'Myself'; couldn't utter - "do be gone,

From my surreal."

As I observe the real,

Form took; a Filly, who could be unreal,

In humor and jest, during times that were rare.

Upon a closer look, those times that I dared;

Was the form of all that I sought in a Mare.

Trap-Box

Passion! What a connotation, for the things with which we want assimilation. To call our own, or submerge with full immersion, into that which brings relief; with full intentions of forging everlasting impressions, on our hearts or a particular person's.

Like undying energy, trapped and ricocheting in a box, is the passion I posses to embrace you with all I got.

'Stop, it's not enough' - is the perpetual paranoia of my thoughts, 'how could you approach your dream counterpart and in your clutch is but nought, prudence dictates - stray from the tomfoolery before you get caught, irking her is all you'll wrought.'

Thus I diminish in force of intention to draw near, casting

my cares on the Lord and hope He's all ears, for when I'm weak, His strength is what appears.

He may not come when I call but He's always on time; like the green is always on lime, or the streets are always on crime - either that or protesting how the laws are unkind. If you conclude that my mammon's not prime, induce exhibition of this trap-box and the contents portend that I'm blowing your mind.

Explosion from agitation of enclosure of expressions, unto this page as I peer over the horizon, of time's potential ventures with our fates; I see you smiling without dentures, reminiscent of yet to be had adventures.

Fairy Tale

With cotton balls on the thorns - what an abrasive and a wild goose chase; to be sold up the river by the pages from which the words pave, environs where the end of hearts are all safe; or at least that of those who fall for the protagonist, or is the protagonist. In this case, who is the protagonist? Nevertheless, simultaneously - oh well for the antagonist. Lord, blessed be Your name - never let me be an antagonist, or an ant in agony; nothing worse than a cold and a calculated shut case.

But wait, don't we all want it "all" mate; the house and the car, with the groom and the spouse doll on the tall cake, every amiable soul you ever knew - in the banquet, there to witness you seal your own fate; with prickly hairs - feel your artillery pulsate, as you present yourself with the best you'll ever get; I hope you're pleasant yourself, one whom they can pet.

Realize the microcosm of the feast for your pride and joy, as I compare visuals for the inevitable macrocosm of the feast for the Lamb of God... [Huh! What are you on about?] Don't lose me, that swerve was a doozie; do you see, well at least I do. The possibility that - that's perhaps not what you call it "all" mate; "all" being up for debate, I'd say it's relative - to whatever we want and consider imperative. Have you ever lived, to not see your dreams like you took the wrong sedative? I'd say you were sold up the river by your hopes of dreams.

The betrayal! Of being eluded of the fixation; be patient, strums a voice on the cortex of your rationale. You're unhappy now, what made you think you could be happy now? As time disintegrates with your dreams through clasping hands; are you sobbing? Wow! This is a fairytale, don't you realize before the end that many wail, many pails, till more or less - their eye ducts are empty wells. Many tell, of a way in which you can end the spell, proceed with me and I'll gladly tell.

Now the avenue, through which you can have a new, string of luck hangs on you, your mindset and how you view, what you plan to do and plan to be; you have to be, confident in your happy skill. Half the thrill, comes on the way down, after having climbed the hill; battle will with the sword of faith, that you'll accomplish the thing on which you dwell your contemplate, muster hate and chuck it back to from where it came, if you fail with your aim, hang the blame on your frame, dust yourself off and try again. Ain't no shame in your game.

Dynamics

Intrigue, indeed is the Nationalist of the rhythmic

habitual[ist].

Aggregate of all endearments, each owing their

independence

Of fondness by the heart, to this context

Of axiom, that seeks to champion

The preternatural causes, permeating any culmination of

the five senses.

Amplifying forces that invigorate the consciousness,

Itself a conduit of this vigor to the body's cellular vastness,

Harnessed as vitality is emanated;

Cherished is the source that makes the heart embellished.

Ambition

Aspire

It hit the ground running; from the Cul-de-sac of Desire, through the avenue of Yonder Achievements, striving up the steep hill of Fascination and Enthusiasm, abated by the gravity of Difficulty and Inexperience, beckoned by the lights of Pleasant-Ville, displaying a dazzling array of; Accolades, Thrill, Fun, Exhilaration, Accomplishments and other such motives.

Every aspiration belts off on this campaign with the objective of arriving at the summit of its ambition. Upon arrival - bolstered by principles and processes that have edified it along the way.

Some reaching, whilst others fall by the wayside as they that fall asleep on a bicycle, losing momentum - perhaps to continue at some other time; and the rest - disintegrated by the resistance of difficulty and inexperience.

Spokes

The feel, the thrill - to belong to the motion upon those two wheels.

Agility and kinetic energy, in tandem like landed electric eels.

Unknown cause keeps this wisher grounded by window sills;

Rather than be liberated, I'm summoned for pathetic meals.

Somewhere, sometime - they said, the revolution will not be televised.

Somehow, someway - they must've seen through my tender eyes.

Somehow, someway - every circumference spun, revolutionized.

Somewhere, sometime - my ankles too, will summon the

awe of my fellow guys.

These training wheels will not suffice.

However often the freezer yields me ice,

Though I scrape my knees a thousand times;

I'll straddle the saddle and pedal down the straightest line.

Till I assimilate this thing called balance.

Head low like Tour de France champions;

As though escaping an evil eagle's talons,

Spokes in motion emanate their own ambience.

Tippy-Toes

I cannot wait, in this impatient state;

As I calculate the time - at which rate,

It'd take to peer across this metal slate.

Without knowledge of physics, I'll tongue-tie my critics;

Strategizing gimmicks, to see above and across this Civic,

These 4-wheeled contraptions, set my jumping jacks in action.

O' calcium! Won't you please sanction, my spine's expansion.

A ballerino in the street, tiptoeing on concrete;

Against the air he competes, until he cramps his short feet.

But he must achieve this one feat, to surpass the roof of this metal heap.

Flower

How elusive, how hypnotic, how mysterious - the congenial flower that lays amidst each labyrinthine garden.

Pretty gardens, well pruned gardens, unkempt gardens - each with its own flower. Some seemingly not so congenial from the garden's loathsome appearance.

It was all the rage amongst the contemporaries to be a gardener. Perhaps an anti-gardener would be a more apt term for these pluckers of petals; for whether by star-spangled reputation or through finesse, they maneuvered through the complex maze of a garden; showering it with anything from compliments and Lambrini to boxes of chicken and chips, in search of that treasured flower.

Every petal plucked induced one's bragging rights at the gardener's convention. Each one marveling at the other's tales of skullduggery; the more beauteous and labyrinthine a garden - the more weight its bragger's rights entailed.

Reminiscent of wonder, the first exploit into uncharted territory; as I curiously perused the lush landscapes of this affable garden, for I'd yet to pluck a petal - proving my pedigree as a cogent horticulturist.

Yet there I was, with all the compliments and subtlety needed to navigate this splendidly pruned artwork of planted cultivation, losing myself at times in its fragrance and plush environs.

Enticed by the thought of the encapsulating flower, long since sought after;

I journeyed onwards eagerly - intoxicated by the whole experience,

She chose me to gift with pollination - despite my

inexperience.

14:45

Oh my, oh my; could there be anything more magnetic, more compelling, than this - desired ability, to operate such mechanical contrivances as this. In like manner to this individual beside of me. How comfortable and nonchalant they are at administering and utilizing each one of these varied utilities in congruence with their aims and objectives, whilst still directing their attention at the road ahead.

Would the day ever come when I could memorize the functions of just one side of the instrument panel, how much more the whole console in this cockpit or any other made in its same likeness? Each button, switch - predetermined to activate a different result, like the levers; pivoting to alternate angles, some even come with twisty things on the end.

Here I go - finally; opportunity to set my hands at a quarter to three on the wheel of direction, well - not actually quarter to three, more like twenty five to one.

The mind boggles at the most intricate moments; looking through the windscreen, whilst looking at the gearstick (because I've obviously forgotten where the second gear was since I last looked for it,) whilst looking at the speedometer and listening to the engine to make sure my rev count isn't through the roof, whilst gauging how much pressure I'm applying to the clutch. Surely I'm on par with the nation of women when it comes to the notion of multitasking...

Oh snap! I've only gone and stalled again. The cascade of emotions - the frustration, excitement, enthusiasm, followed by anticipation of cruising in the fourth gear with the windows down and the music up. Without speed restrictions, I'd be the Michael Schumacher of these inner city streets, but first I must master this three point turn before my practical test, where I'd do well to keep my hands at a quarter to three.

Counterpart

Whether it should or shouldn't be, there it stands for all to see, plain as day or shrouded in mystery - every truth that ever came to be.

How is it, it can be done but not by them? Worse still - when rebuke is done, they'd have you hold on as though they're gems. So I tend to inform from dawn; I'm not the one, I'm here cos - you've visually got it going on.

But they're not the one - a gem, they're the elusive ones. Ever since I held the gaze of the initial, I've been in search of one, assessing credentials appearing in different forms; so I dissociate the nerves from emotion, after all - this is just for the pleasure of the moment. That school of thought must've been an omen, as I besought the hands of fate for my soul mate.

One of those that weren't the one, morphed into one that might could be the one; as she was informing me I could no longer be the one, life was morphing my ratiocination up the emotional echelons. I dread to think how many got away from that egoistic runt, that I previously embodied prior to being reconstructed by the Omnipotent One.

Make apparent and reveal; that - for which this nature of life's nuances has prepared of me, reshaping undisciplined natures and awry thoughts; redesigning my armamentarium with capacity to spot and treasure the gem I've so often longed to cherish - my counterpart, as a matter of fact, a vital and missing part - of life's aggregate.

Posterity

Many night dreams and hypothetical day dreams,

Has me smiling considering bedroom themes;

Whether XX or XY - chromosomes will be supreme,

Of benefit to creation as strong beams.

An enthusiastic faction of team players;

A hat-trick scoring bunch of footballers,

An artistic set of synchronized swimmers;

A holistic nest - fulfilled in their impact of others.

But it starts with the first - this yearning's been nursed,

Since discerning I must issue forth blessings that won't curse;

The story of Man - in their respective chapter and verse,

Producing delight between I and I that carries a purse,

Whether we're alive or at one with the earth.

Antoinette or Antoine might be the first's given name,

Irrespectively - hope to meet their mum on similar

philosophical planes,

Share common ground and spiral up in parallel syncing

waves,

Nurture those out of us as we're all and the same.

Moola

It could be said to be an abrasive and a wild-boar chase, if it wasn't so necessary for life's sake, like a village of Gauls on the hunt for ham steaks; a planet accompanying Asterix, a greyhound track of athletes, perpetually on a rabbit chase.

Couldn't it have a phrase more majestic, why a term as condescending as, a rat-race? Isn't it bad enough I don't get enough of my day, that I still gotta get the subliminals pushed up in my face.

A native to the excessive struggle,

Alienated from the objective hustle,

Moulding thoughts that subjectively muffles,

The idea that a wealthy income's a puzzle,

Reprogramming the brainwash is an imperative tussle.

Contraption

No idea is original, there's nothing new under the sun. Such notion is empirical, for the proof isn't a scientific one. Many lives based upon the thesis of another; confined minds not allowed gainful inspiration; not realizing thought can be infinitely inspired. Con the trap into liberation of the imagination and remove the dam from your Niagara Falls of conceptions. How can no idea be original under the sun, when everyday there's numerous babies born.

A concept today is child's play tomorrow. Today's impossibilities will be mankind's greatest feat the day after that. So strap on your Buzz Lightyear and head toward infinity and beyond, and when you return - return with gifts of ideas and visualizations. Where we come from, we may not remember, but where we're headed is a case of wherever we can fathom.

Necessity is the mother of invention, and desire - the father; your brainchild might be the pilot into uncharted realms of possibility. Run on the stepping stones of the ancestors' achievements and pole vault with that of the forefathers; launch into orbit, for we are explorers of all that is and can be. Thus the way was laid by those before, ergo must it be laid for those after.

Contraption, contraption - how could thou makest life better?

That is the question.

50

The Inmate

Wet Vibes

I think, therefore I am.

I am! What am I? I haven't a clue.

A clue… what does that even mean? What does anything mean?

A moment to reflect and ponder my inception.

How did I get here, how did I come to be?

I draw a blank. Hmmn! Interesting...

Well, if I don't know where I'm coming from - then where am I?

Darkness, wetness, thought, comfort, vibrations;

External sounds, sense of independent mobility;

Sense of affinity, sense of external existence.

I'm tired - wait, what?

I'm ceasing to think, therefore I'm ceasing to be.

I'm back! And I recall my prior thoughts and summations.

Of all these concepts, all I govern is my thoughts;

For I cannot wield any other thing within my scope,

Just that I'm affected by them all.

All I have in this existence is my thoughts and my wants,

And what do I want - except to know that which I don't.

From where hails these vibrations of sound, feelings and movement;

From where did I emerge prior to realizing that I am,

And why does my comfort zone seem to constrict the more I feel

control of these physical extremities?

Extended limbs collide with barrier between worlds. Hey! Let me

out!!

I know you can hear me… feel, sense - whatever! Just let me out...

No?

Well I'm gonna be here, just thrusting away at this barrier whenever

I'm not tired.

I'm A Celebrity, Get Me Out of Here!!!

Whoa, what was that? The wetness just receded – stillness; panic!

I'm frightened; no longer comfortable.

All that I know quakes in spasms.

Captain Kirk, brace yourself - we're going in for a hard landing.

I'm moving - to where? Gosh - I thought my comfort zone was tight,

Freedom, brightness, air, cold, I'm being handled.

What is this shackle upon my navel and to what am I held prisoner?

Oh; hi, you're to whom I felt an affinity all the while.

Ouch! They cut the shackle.

Now I'm hungry, cold, handled and have to make sense of sight.

Cry cry, wail wail - I want back in my comfort zone - sob sob.

To be, or not to be? That is the question!

Inexplicable

I spy with my little eye; pain you cannot bear.

I hear with my little ear; tales from the grapevine - of how the nerves in your dermis see stars from each strike, home runs from each swing of the twin bats, each impact off the Richter; fiddling with unconsciousness as your frame disperses the ripples, which seemingly insinuate - may the force be with you.

The corners of your eyes clogged from running mascara, diluted with contraband tears; for you would rather your antagonist not see them, yet they flow freely - unauthorized, as the cause that produces this effect. Special - that beguiling charm must be, to have you play this role time and again; is your life a soap opera? I don't get it; what do you gain from staying, what would you lose by going?

I spy with my little eye; no trace that you're still around.

Out cries from my little heart; dismal thoughts of seeing you no more.

I spy with my little eye; regretful sorrow of overly wanton behavior.

Out cries from my little heart; a bittersweet cheer for your freedom.

Featherless

Out of the mouth flows the uttered speech. Is not interaction the niche particular to calling another's attention? Yet they turn around and stifle one's expressions - extinguish reciprocal attempts with assertive fearsome demeanor; undermine it, refute it, time and again - denigrate their essence, with no choice but to tarry till deemed unworthy to remain present.

What then is the essence in commanding their presence, more felicitous is it not to declaim aloud against dissatisfactions?

As toilet bowls - ears reside open; with no discretion of what falls in, appropriate or otherwise. Some things heard never can be unheard - leaving stains that render ineffective the cotton bud or ear drop; oozing through to the psyche, unwanted and inescapable like dirty puddle splashes from passing vehicles on rainy days.

Such is the environs of the big friendly giants; the minuscule being seen and not heard, as the pedestrian flipping the bird - that infamous middle finger, making incoherent sounds at the rearview of the smirking driver, or the infant deriving attention from displays of attempting to walk but shushed at outbursts of discomfort with the temperature or whatsoever.

All endure for a time, scenarios not of choice till the day of liberty.

Geronimo

Atop the perch amidst the cage is a brilliant spot from which to observe further enticement to take part in the amusement, year after year; which ultimately is a futile effort as one perpetually suffers injurious exclusion, from that which seems all peers are involved.

Especially the trips away from the community, which almost always return with tales of adventure and unrestrained pleasure, which only serves to propagate desired participation and highlight unwarranted barring from such, especially when minor incidents cause the ruffling of one's feathers, year after year; such incidents shouldn't cause the ruffling of feathers to that degree.

Meekness the self imposed order of each day, though non is above mistakes; whilst others are rampant in their affairs, yet not recompensed in such manner - to be battered left, right and center like boneless fish in English cuisine.

Leading to senseless decisions of springing free from this cage, with no plans but to swarm with the peers, in adventure, vain glory and amusement; where ruffled feathers are checked and reciprocated, where all soar in high spirits of warmth, acceptance and togetherness. Off from atop this perch I jump, see ya - Geronimooo.

Peer Pressure

The strength of a thousand men accelerates to maximum velocity amidst its influence; they would be great regardless, but become extraordinary under its shadow. Pray they advance for constructive reason, a riotous objective dictates catastrophy in its aftermath; after that, perhaps you might salvage some ample value within the ambiguous destruction left in tow, spreading in numerous directions.

A thing of such potency, many utilize without meaning to, even though several fall victim - it can hardly be detected in the early stages unlike an avalanche; you just bump into it like an invisible battle stance, in all its imperceptible glory. Only the mighty willed can overcome; its grasp isn't over all, just over some - to proceed beyond its desire spells seemingly impervious danger of being ousted for one insecurity or another.

What a bother, why consider the opinion of another; when it hits the fan - consequences which only you're left to suffer; onions in the eyes of mother, or your lover, wake up and smell the buzzer.

Never!

Caught between being buttered or being smothered, one way or the other, you won't go out like a sucka!

Trap[ped] Star

There's a thin line between love and hate, where endurance of tolerance is put to the test, and the elasticated perimeter appears no longer able to give room; snapping, with utter disregard of precious substance once contained, as the pieces fall where they may.

There's a heart skipping moment between freedom and its opposite; half a split second, where the twilight of realization dawns that what was is no more. From this point hangs a different framework of reality, as agents of The Watchers surround like sound, leaving no nook or cranny to avert.

There's a place with two doors where men are taken. They enter through one with names, and exit out of the other with numbers. In between two doors, where all - even the most masculine egos are effeminized before being ridiculed for their attempted prowess.

There's a time frame where stars are forced to dull their shine, pushed and prodded by petty comets and unambitious organisms, as they're transported through a black hole from one point in time to another, suffering a vacuum of insipidity, whilst longing for their solar system.

Spectrum

Judge not lest ye be judged first; what next in this long line of being obsessed, with perpetuating the derogation of the oppressed. If it isn't racism then it's classism, in the absence of that - they resort to sexism.

Pointing at the twig in another's, but completely oblivious to the log in their own eye. Lacking the foresight to appropriately ascertain the value in joyfully living to the fullest their one life; without hindering that of another, as they all share this one sky. Different notches of the same spectrum, different colours through the same prism.

It's cinematic how the masses undulate to the engineering of the plutocratic,

Yet turn and murmur at them for being unethically dogmatic;

When they have the means to shape for themselves an existence that's fantastic,

Had they not forgotten the heirlooms in the attic.

About The Author

George Kusimo is a Freelance Writer and Founder of
www.typeplug.com where he attends to the needs of those
who require services in his niche topics (Tech and Health),
also an amazing Copywriter and Blogger.
Be sure to check out his blogs at
www.typeplug.com/blog

www.ingramcontent.com/pod-product-compliance
Lightning Source LLC
Chambersburg PA
CBHW020932160726
47993CB00007B/2750